EXPLORING
FORMATIVE
ASSESSMENT

SERIES

EXPLORING
FORMATIVE
ASSESSMENT

Susan M. Brookhart

Alexandria, Virginia USA

ASCD®

Association for Supervision and Curriculum Development
1703 N. Beauregard St. • Alexandria, VA 22311-1714 USA
Phone: 800-933-2723 or 703-578-9600 • Fax: 703-575-5400
Web site: www.ascd.org • E-mail: member@ascd.org
Author guidelines: www.ascd.org/write

Gene R. Carter, *Executive Director*; Nancy Modrak, *Publisher*; Julie Houtz, *Director of Book Editing & Production*; Leah Lakins, *Project Manager*; Catherine Guyer, *Senior Graphic Designer*; Mike Kalyan, *Production Manager*; Marlene Hochberg, *Typesetter*; Sarah Plumb, *Production Specialist*

Printed in the United States of America. Cover art copyright © 2009 by ASCD. ASCD publications present a variety of viewpoints. The views expressed or implied in this book should not be interpreted as official positions of the Association.

PAPERBACK ISBN: 978-1-4166-0826-4   ASCD product #: 109038   n4/09
Also available as an e-book through ebrary, netLibrary, and many online booksellers (see Books in Print for the ISBNs).

Quantity discounts for the paperback edition only: 10–49 copies, 10%; 50+ copies, 15%; for 1,000 or more copies, call 800-933-2723, ext. 5634, or 703-575-5634. For desk copies: member@ascd.org.

Library of Congress Cataloging-in-Publication Data

Brookhart, Susan M.
  Exploring formative assessment / Susan Brookhart.
    p. cm. – (The professional learning community series)
  Includes bibliographical references and index.
  ISBN 978-1-4166-0826-4 (pbk. : alk. paper) 1. Teachers–In-service training. 2. Educational tests and measurements. 3. Group work in education. 4. Teachers' workshops. I. Title.

  LB1731.B728 2009
  371.26–dc22

                          2008055542
_____

20 19 18 17 16 15 14 13 12 11 10 09   1 2 3 4 5 6 7 8 9 10 11 12

Exploring Formative Assessment

Section I

Creating a
Professional Learning Community

Welcome to an adventure! If you are a teacher who is interested in developing your classroom repertoire and increasing your students' achievement and motivation, you are in for a treat. Professional learning communities are a vehicle for connecting and improving teacher practice and student outcomes. Formative assessment is an approach to assessment and instruction that increases both students' motivation and achievement. Before we launch into the logistics, the how-to's, and the work involved in professional learning communities, it's important to focus on this promise of adventure. Joining this adventure is why you are here and part of this professional learning community. Welcome!

How is a professional learning community defined? In this workbook, a professional learning community (or PLC) is defined as a group of four to six teachers or administrators who do the following:

- Meet regularly
- Work on shared goals and related tasks between meetings
- Accomplish shared goals

For this workbook, the shared goals will be

- Increasing teacher knowledge and skill in formative assessment
- Increasing student motivation and achievement

Let's begin our discussion by looking at each component of a PLC.

Why should a PLC include only four to six participants? The number of participants in a PLC can be flexible; however, the group needs to be large enough so that group members can contribute a variety of perspectives and experiences and small enough to allow each group member's work to be discussed. If your group includes an even number of participants, colleagues can work in pairs between sessions. Working in pairs has added benefits for the group because it will decrease the number of projects that are discussed at any one time, and it will increase the options available for working on the projects. For example, two teachers can try the same strategy in their classrooms, observe each other, and reflect on the strategy in the context of two different teachers and groups of students.

Why is it important to meet regularly and work between meetings? A PLC is a group in which teachers work collaboratively to reflect on their practice. The group examines evidence about the relationship between teacher practices and student outcomes. This work will require time for discussion and work between meetings to read informational pieces, reflect on them, try new things in the classroom, and collect evidence about the results. Meeting without anything meaty to discuss is pointless. Reading and classroom work without taking the time to reflect, share, and learn from them are also pointless. An effective PLC will require both meetings and work to be successful.

What can you expect to happen as a result of your work in a PLC? When PLCs function well, they accomplish more than just the specific teaching and learning goals that the members of the PLC set out to investigate. First and foremost, changes should improve teaching and learning for students. According to McLaughlin and Talbert (2006), results from learning communities in schools include the following:

- Teachers build and manage various kinds of knowledge, such as knowledge about content and pedagogy and the skills to use this knowledge in practice.
- Teachers and administrators develop a shared language and shared standards for practice and student outcomes.
- Teachers and administrators sustain vital aspects of school culture. Learning together becomes a schoolwide value.

In your PLC, you will be building shared language and shared standards of practice in formative assessment. You will be developing a classroom and school climate in which mistakes and successes are opportunities to learn and learning is more about increasing students' understanding of a topic than about helping them earn good grades.

Recruiting

If you are reading this workbook, you may have already made a commitment to become a member of a PLC that is focused on investigating formative assessment. Where will you find others interested in such a commitment? Here are three strategies that may help you. Select the strategy that is most appropriate for your situation.

- **Ask people.** Your school or district may already have groups that meet regularly. A smaller group within an existing group may decide they have a mutual interest in investigating formative assessment. Building principals and other district administrators are good sources for lists of names. See if any of the people on the lists are interested in joining a PLC focused on investigating formative assessment, and ask if they have suggestions for other educators you might contact. Work with administrators on logistics for your PLC meetings. Administrators should be able to help you with needs for time, space, and other resources. They should know whether it is possible to arrange for release time or plan for other contractual benefits that will allow teachers and other administrators to participate in the PLC.

- **Make announcements or distribute flyers**. Ask for time at a faculty meeting or other gathering to make an informational announcement so that you can begin recruiting members for your PLC. Prepare for that announcement by writing down the goals for the PLC. The announcement should include why the PLC is important, what you expect participants to do during the PLC experience, and what you expect the benefits will be. Communicate your excitement and interest. Give as many details as you can and also stress that some of the details will be worked out collaboratively at the first meeting. Finally, distribute a handout with a summary of the information and contact information that will allow teachers and administrators to follow-up with you and indicate their interests (see Figure 1 on p. 4) This handout can be distributed in school mailboxes to those who were not present at the meeting.

- **Hold an open house**. Identify a time and place for an open-house style meeting to explore the PLC as an option. Invite people to the meeting by inquiring or distributing flyers and specify that it will be an informational meeting only. Use all or some of the materials from Session 1A (see pp. 12–17) to introduce the topic of formative assessment so people can make an informed decision about whether they would like to participate. Decide whether you will ask for a decision about participation at the end of the meeting or by a certain time in the future. Make sure those who attend the meeting know how they should communicate with you to indicate whether or not they would like to participate.

Meeting Basics

Organizing your meeting should include attention to scheduling, attendance, roles, and ground rules.

Scheduling

How often will you meet? Where will you meet? When? Two recommended patterns for meetings are as follows:

- **Once a month**. There are seven topics and session activities, plus an evaluation and wrap-up that would allow you to meet once a month. This schedule would give you plenty of time in between meetings to read, reflect, try things in your classroom, and collect student evidence.

FIGURE 1

Sample Meeting Flyer

YOU ARE INVITED!

What: Join a professional learning community to investigate formative assessment

Who: A group of 4 to 6 teachers and administrators who are committed to studying and trying out formative assessment strategies in the classroom.

This group will meet regularly and work between meetings to achieve the following goals:
- Increase our knowledge and skill in formative assessment
- Increase student motivation and achievement.

Where:

Our first meeting is:

For additional information:

RSVP by:

- **Twice a month.** In once-a-month meetings, your group will not have an exhaustive discussion for each topic, and the group will not have time to process all the teacher reflections and student work. You might choose to meet twice a month or every two weeks, using the first session of each month to review readings and do content-based activities. The second session could be used to discuss reports of classroom activities and student work.

Attendance

It would be wise to have an explicit expectation that all members commit to attending all sessions, except for emergencies. Attendance is important both for the continuity of content and for the creation of a group atmosphere that fosters open discussion.

Roles

Your group should specifically decide to have one or two facilitators. At each meeting, the facilitator should assign any other cooperative roles (e.g., recorder or discussion leader) and any homework roles and responsibilities for the next meeting. The following list includes descriptions for roles within the PLC.

- **Logistical facilitator.** Each group needs at least one logistical facilitator or coordinator who will send meeting reminders, set agendas, reserve space, and attend to any other logistics as needed (e.g., collecting materials or making copies of readings).
- **Meeting facilitator.** Each group also needs a meeting facilitator who keeps meetings moving, monitors participation, and ensures that each member adheres to the ground rules. This meeting facilitator role may be performed by the same person who handles the logistics.
- **Discussion leader.** Within various session activities, a discussion leader and the content for discussion should be mutually agreed on before the next meeting. For example, if a group member commits to trying a particular formative assessment practice in her classroom, that person would be responsible for bringing and presenting the appropriate reflections and student work to the next meeting. She would also report on what she did, call on her partner/observer to explain what she saw, and bring any questions that she wanted to discuss to the group. Every group member should have this responsibility at least once a year.
- **Recorder.** It is a good idea to have a recorder to take notes on the discussion. This role can be permanent or it can rotate depending on the wishes of your group.

Ground Rules

Have a discussion at the beginning of the first meeting about ground rules for group meetings. Try to establish general expectations that will help build an open and inquiry-oriented community. Avoid narrow rules. Your group will decide on its own ground rules but consider these following ground rules as possibilities. Easton (2008) and McLaughlin and Talbert (2006) have found the following ground rules to be characteristics of successful professional learning communities:

- **Develop an ethic of sharing**. There should be plenty of room for everyone to share in the group. PLCs are not a zero-sum game. If one person gets time, energy, or commitment, another person should not lose his or her opportunity to contribute to the group. Group members should also develop an ethic of commitment to share their time, energy, and resources for the good of the group.
- **Allow group members to ask questions**. If a group member asks "Why?" or "How do you know that?," you should not view it as a personal challenge. Questioning is the hallmark of an inquiry approach. There is no learning without wondering.
- **Invite other teachers into the classroom**. Peer observation will give you a second pair of eyes to look at what you are doing. Peer observation will help verify your successes and provide feedback for practices that could be improved. Peer observation should be done in a nonjudgmental fashion.
- **Do not say "I already do that" as a first response**. For example, teachers often say they already share their learning targets with students or give clear feedback. It is a matter of inquiry to discover how students understand learning targets and feedback and how such practices can be improved or tailored to specific student needs. The first response to any topic should be "Let's see what we can find out about that."

Creating Effective Agendas

Most meetings will have an agenda similar to the agenda shown in Figure 2. The first meeting agenda (see Sessions 1A and 1B on pp. 12–23) will be different. Each meeting should end with setting the agenda for the next meeting and a "What did I learn today?" wrap-up session.

Agenda Topics

Work between Sessions

You can see from Figure 2 that the between-session work is crucial to the success of the PLC. The meat of the meetings — the discussion of readings, sharing and reflecting on

FIGURE 2

Sample Meeting Agenda

- **Introduction** (The facilitator leads this section.)
  - The facilitator reviews the roles and expectations for the meeting.
  - The facilitator reviews the agenda for the day.
- **Previous Topic Homework** (All group members participate.)
  - Discussion of readings
  - Sharing and reflecting on classroom experiences and reviewing student work (The discussion leader presents information and leads discussion.)
- **New Topic** (The facilitator leads this section.)
  - Introduction of new topic (facilitator responsible)
  - Shared language: Discussion of a new term (facilitator leads, optional except for Session 1A)
  - Identify what to read and reflect on before next meeting
  - Make commitments about classroom activities all will try and who will be responsible for presenting and leading the discussion at the next meeting
  - If pairs are not permanent features of your group, identify who will work with whom for classroom trials
- **Wrap-up** (The facilitator leads this section.)
  - What did I learn?

classroom experiences, and reviewing student work — is in the first and second bullets. Participants must have read the assigned materials, reflected on them, and bring questions or points for discussion to the session in order for the discussion to lead to insights and learning for the group. Additionally, participants must also try formative assessment ideas in their classrooms, collect student work, be observed by a colleague, and reflect on their work. Simply put, what you get out of the PLC is what you put into it.

However, this exhortation isn't an "eat-your-spinach" sort of rule. Participants should find the readings interesting and the classroom work fun. As McLaughlin and Talbert (2006) pointed out, the feeling of "doing extra work" should dissipate as teachers begin to see changes in their students' work. The process should become more self-motivating as time goes on.

About three-quarters of your time will be spent on between-session activities. Suggested readings and reflection questions are provided for each session topic. Groups may also want to locate and read other resources. If additional readings are not assigned by group consensus, they may become options or suggested readings.

Joint Work between Sessions

Participants can only try out formative assessment practices and collect evidence about their use in the classroom. Working in pairs is strongly recommended. This can be done in two ways. Two teachers may wish to try out the same formative assessment practices, observe each other and their students, and reflect jointly on what they have learned. Each member of a pair may also wish to experiment with a different practice, be an external observer, and share ideas. When partners can find areas of common interest, joint work on similar practices has proven to be a very powerful method (McLaughlin & Talbert, 2006).

Reflection

Reflecting is a more focused activity than the term implies. Reflections on reading should start with comprehension (i.e., "What were the author's main points?" or "What do these points have to do with formative assessment in general and with this session's topic in particular?") Next, you should make connections with your own work (i.e., "What do I already do that is something like this?" or "What might be a growing edge of practice for me?") Reflections on classroom activities are more than general thoughts about what worked or went well. First, and often overlooked, reflect on exactly what you did. Sometimes classroom teaching goes according to plan and sometimes it gets modified on the floor. Second, reflect on the assumptions behind what you did. What did you think would happen? Why did you select that activity? What were the thoughts behind your choices for choosing a specific principle of learning or student development? What did you think about the content you were teaching? Third, reflect on what the students did. How did they act during the lesson? What did they say individually or in discussion? What sort of work did they produce? What was the quality? Finally, after you have drawn conclusions about what you learned from what actually happened, run any what-if scenarios in your mind. For example, ask yourself, "What if I had asked the students to do this?" or "What if I had given them more time to do something?" or "What if I had given them different instructions or materials?"

It is also strongly recommended that you keep a journal while you are participating in a PLC. In addition to responding to the specific reflection questions for each reading or activity, you will want to process the whole experience as you go. What stands out in your mind? What insights surprised you? Date each entry and jot down your thoughts. Try to do this at least after each session. Weekly entries will allow you to have even more opportunities to write about your classroom-based insights.

Classroom Connections

Two classroom connection activities are suggested for each topic area — an introductory-level and an experienced-level activity. In general, choose the introductory-level activity if you have not done much classroom inquiry work in the specific topic area. Choose the experienced-level activity if you have already done some classroom inquiry work in the specific topic and want to extend your learning. There may be some exceptions based on a particular classroom situation.

Potential Stumbling Blocks

Be aware of the potential stumbling blocks that can derail PLCs and keep them from being productive and satisfying. Easton (2008) and McLaughlin and Talbert (2006) have identified these points in research. Knowing about these challenges before you begin your work should help you manage them and keep your PLC on track.

Time

Time is always an issue in schools. Before there is evidence of student improvement from PLC work, it may seem like an add-on or just something else to do. Research has shown that once teachers begin to see changes in student work arising from their own professional learning, the investment of time seems worthwhile (McLaughlin & Talbert, 2006). Plus, as the work becomes more a part of your professional routine, it will seem less like an extra activity.

Participants' Beliefs about Students

Participants' beliefs about students, content and pedagogy, professional norms, and collegial relationships have a lot to do with the success of a PLC. For example, if you don't believe the PLC work is important, you won't put your best effort into it and won't get much out of it. Two important beliefs about students and pedagogy are individual and collective efficacy.

Individual teacher efficacy involves embracing two related beliefs: first, that teaching can make a difference, and second, that you personally can make a difference in students' learning. Believe it or not, there are teachers who don't think school can make much of a difference. It will not surprise you to find out that these teachers are not as effective as the teachers who do believe they can make a difference. Collective efficacy is a similar concept that focuses on a school-level team. It's the belief that together the educators who create the learning climate in a building can make a difference in the lives and learning of their students. In both cases, it's about real belief. It's not enough to know that the right answer is "I can make a difference." Real efficacy shows through in actions.

Two other potential stumbling blocks that individual teachers may have less control over are resource allocation and school and class policies. Before or during your PLC work, if you find that there are resources or policy issues that you can fix and will help you work better, see what you can do to improve them. There are some budget, schedule, and policy issues that are set, and there are some issues that can be changed if you ask and make a good case.

Section II

Session 1
What is Formative Assessment?

Introduction

Session 1 is divided in two parts. Part A can be done as an open-house session for recruiting teachers or administrators who might be interested in becoming part of a PLC focused on studying formative assessment. If this session is an open house, only do Part A, and request that participants think about their interest and respond with a commitment by a certain date and time. You can use Part B during the first official PLC meeting. If the teachers and administrators in attendance have already committed to participating in the PLC, use Part A as an orientation meeting.

Goals for Session 1

1. Understand the concept of formative assessment.
2. Develop a shared understanding of the PLC structure and participant responsibilities.

Preparation

1. If this is an open-house session and the participants do not have copies of this booklet, the facilitator will make copies of the following pages:

- Session 1A Agenda (pp. 12–13)
- What is Formative Assessment? (pp. 14)
- Shared Language: What is Formative Assessment? (p. 15)
- Classroom Connections Options (p. 16)

2. The facilitator should be familiar with and prepared to lead the session.
3. For Session 1B, the facilitator should make copies of the following article: Chappuis, S., & Chappuis, J. (2008, January). The best value in formative assessment. *Educational Leadership*, 65(4), 14-18.

Handout 1.1
Session 1A Agenda

Introduction (The facilitator leads this section.)

- The facilitator opens the meeting with personal introductions and asks participants to include why they came and what they want to get out of the session.
- The facilitator introduces the topic by using the informational handout "What is Formative Assessment?" (p. 14).

Discuss the First Topic (Shared Understanding of Formative Assessment)

- Using the Shared Language worksheet on p. 15, ask the participants to complete the worksheet individually, discuss it in pairs, and report out to the group.

Orientation to the PLC Structure

- The facilitator announces that the content or "meat" of each session begins with three inputs from this book: (1) shared language activities (optional except for the first one on formative assessment), (2) assigned readings and reflection questions, and (3) classroom connection activities, including reflections and student work.
- The facilitator distributes the Classroom Connections Options handout on p. 16. The facilitator should explain how the Classroom Connections activities can be used. Each session presents prescribed Classroom Connections activities, but participants may substitute their own choices from this list. Participants must bring back both their reflections and evidence of the effects on their students when it is their turn to present to the group.
- The facilitator sets the roles and ground rules using the Meeting Basics on pp. 3–6. If this meeting is an open-house session, use this section as additional information for your gathering. If this session is an orientation to an existing PLC, have a brief discussion about whether each member can commit to these roles and ground rules. Decide on what sort of roles your group will need, seek volunteers, and assign people accordingly.

Wrap-up (a)

- If this meeting is an open-house session, conclude with a brief sharing session with the group. Answer any questions, and tell people how and when they should indicate whether they would be interested in participating in the PLC.

Wrap-up (b)

- If this is an orientation session for an existing PLC, assign the reading for Session 1B. Participants will finish this reading and complete the Reflections on Reading worksheet on p. 17 before Session 1B.
- Set the next meeting date.
- Decide who will be the facilitator for Session 1B.
- Decide who will be responsible for leading the reading discussion at Session 1B.

Handout 1.2
What is Formative Assessment?

Formative assessment refers to the ongoing process both students and teachers engage in when they

- Focus on learning goals
- Take stock of current student work in relation to the learning goals using formal or informal assessment processes
- Take action to move students closer to the learning goals (i.e., teachers adjust teaching methods or students adjust learning methods)

From a teacher's perspective, formative assessment can involve the following actions:

- Clearly communicating learning goals to students
- Helping students make connections between the learning goals and the work they do
- Getting information from students about where they are
- Giving feedback to students or suggestions about how they might move closer to their learning goals
- Keeping records that show patterns in the kinds of feedback students need and receive
- Facilitating student self-assessment and goal-setting
- Using assessment information to fine-tune lessons in progress and plan future lessons

Teacher skills required for formative assessment include the following:

- Having a clear idea of the learning goal and ways for students to make progress on it
- Using observational skills
- Using verbal skills to give clear feedback
- Developing a repertoire of strategies for teaching the learning goal
- Building a repertoire of motivational strategies

Benefits to students can include the following:

- Increased achievement
- Increased understanding of how to learn
- Increased control over their own learning and increased motivation

Worksheet 1.1
Shared Language: What is Formative Assessment?

Definition

What does the term *formative assessment* mean to you?

What do you wonder about *formative assessment*?

Example and counterexample

Give an example of something you would consider *formative assessment*. Explain why.

Give an example of something you would not consider *formative assessment*. Explain why.

Sharing and focusing

With a partner, share your definitions, examples, and counterexamples. How did you fine-tune your concept of *formative assessment* based on your discussion?

In the whole group, share the results of your partner discussions. As a group, discuss and decide on a current working definition of *formative assessment* and write it below.

Handout 1.3
Classroom Connections Options

Classroom Connections are suggested activities for you to try in your classroom. Activities will be suggested at the introductory and experienced level. For each session topic, select the activity that fits your level of experience with the topic or your interest. If the suggested session activities are not completely in line with your own learning goals, you may design something for yourself. Your self-designed Classroom Connection should be related to the session topic, and you should have good answers for the *before* and *after* questions below.

Classroom Connections activities can be as follows:

1. Strategies and evidence about their implementation and results
2. Student achievement data
3. Student work and/or your feedback
4. Action research
5. Assessment design
6. Case study of a lesson or instructional activity
7. Case study of a student
8. Observations or classroom walk-through visits with a partner
9. Students' voices via interviews, discussions, and questionnaires

Questions to answer before the Classroom Connections activities:

1. What am I interested in? Why?
2. What do I want to know?
3. Where will I get more information?
4. What will I try in my classroom?
5. What are my working assumptions behind deciding to try this?
6. What do I expect to happen?
7. What evidence would it take to convince me that this did or did not happen and to what degree?
8. How will I collect that evidence?

Questions to answer after the Classroom Connections activities:

1. What did I learn? What do I want my colleagues to learn?
2. How will I summarize my evidence to make a case for my colleagues at the next meeting?
3. What questions do I have for my colleagues as they review my evidence?
4. What actions should I take based on this learning?
5. What actions would I like my colleagues to take (e.g., observe, help with data, or try something themselves)?

Worksheet 1.2
Reflections on Reading: What is Formative Assessment?

Read the article "The best value in formative assessment." Answer the reflection questions individually and take your answers to your next PLC session to share your thoughts.

1. According to the authors, what is the difference between formative and summative assessment?

2. Describe some of the summative assessment practices you use in your school or classroom. Do any of them lend themselves to the possibility of being used formatively? If so, how?

3. Describe some of the formative assessment practices you use in your classroom. In particular, describe how you involve the students in answering the three formative questions: Where am I going? Where am I now? How can I close the gap?

4. When are you most likely to give descriptive feedback? Have you ever collected any information about how students in your classes use your descriptive feedback?

5. What interested you the most about this article?

Reference

Chappuis, S., & Chappuis, J. (2008, January). The best value in formative assessment. *Educational Leadership, 65*(4), 14-18.

Handout 1.4
Session 1B Agenda

Introduction (The facilitator leads this section.)

- The facilitator opens the meeting with a welcome and a personal greeting.
- The facilitator reminds the participants of their shared definition of formative assessment from the last session, and makes a note that it will be revisited after the discussion of the reading.

Complete the Pre-Assessment survey

- All participants will complete the Pre-Assessment Questionnaire worksheet individually (see Figure 3 on pp. 19–20) and save it for future use.

Discuss the Reading (All group members participate in this section.)

- Using the Reflections on Reading worksheet on p. 17, all participants will share their insights and questions from the reading, first in pairs and then with the whole group.
- All participants will make adjustments to the group's working definition of formative assessment as needed.

Select Classroom Connection activities for trial between Sessions 1B and 2.

- All participants will review and discuss the Classroom Connections for Formative Assessment on pp. 21 and 22–23. Participants should commit to what they are going to do and why. This planning will allow participants to select partners and build mutual support between meetings. The process will also help the participants to set group expectations for the next meetings. All participants will do the Classroom Connection activities, and one or two group members will volunteer to present their work and questions for discussion at session 2.

Wrap-up (The facilitator leads this section.)
The wrap-up session can be done in either of the following ways:

- The facilitator leads a round-robin discussion where each participant states his or her most salient learning point from the session
- Each participant uses a 3x5 index card to write down one salient learning point from this session and one item that is still fuzzy or incomplete. The facilitator collects the cards and leads a discussion based on the feedback.

Set Next Meeting Date and Responsibilities

- The group will decide who will be the meeting facilitator and the discussion leader for the Classroom Connections at session 2.

FIGURE 3

___

Pre-Assessment Questionnaire

Before you begin your PLC work in formative assessment, circle the choice that best represents how you feel about each of the topics. There are no right or wrong answers. Keep this questionnaire. You will use it for reflection at the end of the sessions.

Using formative assessment in my regular classroom practice			
How much do I know about this?	a lot	a little	not much
How skilled am I at doing this?	very	somewhat	not very
How often do I do this?	routinely	sometimes	not often
How important is this to me?	very	somewhat	not very
How interested am I in learning more about this?	very	somewhat	not very
Setting and sharing goals for students' learning			
How much do I know about this?	a lot	a little	not much
How skilled am I at doing this?	very	somewhat	not very
How often do I do this?	routinely	sometimes	not often
How important is this to me?	very	somewhat	not very
How interested am I in learning more about this?	very	somewhat	not very
Soliciting and listening to students' comments, answers, questions, or problems related to learning goals			
How much do I know about this?	a lot	a little	not much
How skilled am I at doing this?	very	somewhat	not very
How often do I do this?	routinely	sometimes	not often
How important is this to me?	very	somewhat	not very
How interested am I in learning more about this?	very	somewhat	not very
Providing effective feedback on student work			
How much do I know about this?	a lot	a little	not much
How skilled am I at doing this?	very	somewhat	not very
How often do I do this?	routinely	sometimes	not often
How important is this to me?	very	somewhat	not very
How interested am I in learning more about this?	very	somewhat	not very
Asking questions that encourage students to think			
How much do I know about this?	a lot	a little	not much
How skilled am I at doing this?	very	somewhat	not very
How often do I do this?	routinely	sometimes	not often
How important is this to me?	very	somewhat	not very
How interested am I in learning more about this?	very	somewhat	not very

(con't)

Encouraging student self-regulation			
How much do I know about this?	a lot	a little	not much
How skilled am I at doing this?	very	somewhat	not very
How often do I do this?	routinely	sometimes	not often
How important is this to me?	very	somewhat	not very
How interested am I in learning more about this?	very	somewhat	not very
Using formative assessment information in instructional planning			
How much do I know about this?	a lot	a little	not much
How skilled am I at doing this?	very	somewhat	not very
How often do I do this?	routinely	sometimes	not often
How important is this to me?	very	somewhat	not very
How interested am I in learning more about this?	very	somewhat	not very

Worksheet 1.3
Classroom Connections: Formative Assessment
Introductory Level

Identify things you already do in your classroom that are formative in nature. These are potential areas for fine-tuning your Classroom Connections projects. Consider your students' formative assessment questions as you complete this activity.

What aspect of my teaching help students know "Where am I going?"
What aspect of my teaching help students know "How close is my current achievement or performance"
What aspect of my teaching help students know "What do I do next?"

Collect student work and/or peer observations that give evidence for your statements. Explain how the evidence supports the formative nature of your teaching.

What did you learn about your teaching? Which of these aspects of your teaching would be a good launching point for trying a formative assessment practice in-depth?

Worksheet 1.4
Classroom Connections: Formative Assessment
Experienced Level

Do a case study of a student with whom you have worked formatively.

1. What was the learning goal(s) you were working on?

2. How did you communicate the goal(s) to the student?

3. How do you know that he or she understood the goal (e.g., What did the student do, say, or produce that showed understanding)?

4. Describe the student's initial work on this goal. What was the assignment? Attach the work and your feedback. How did the student know what to do next?

5. Describe the student's subsequent work on this goal. What was the assignment? Attach the work and your feedback. What evidence is there that the student used the previous feedback in this work? How did the student know what to do next? If there are other practice assignments, repeat this question.

6. Describe the student's final work on this goal. What was the assignment? Attach the work and your feedback.

7. What was the student's response to the final assignment?

8. What was your next learning goal for this student? How did you and the student select it?

9. What did you learn from assembling this case study? What are your next steps with this student?

Introduction

The first step in formative assessment is being clear about learning goals.

- For the teacher, formative assessment means clearly conveying what you want students to learn, knowing typical student steps and missteps toward this goal (i.e., the typical learning progression), and using assignments that match the learning goal. The latter is very important because it is in the assignment that you translate the learning goal into action for the student. The student will strive to do the assignment, not the abstract goal.
- For the student, formative assessment means understanding the learning goal and knowing what good work looks like. It's not a goal if the student can't envision it.

Goals for Session 2

1. Understand the importance of sharing goals with the students so that they can incorporate the goals into their learning processes.
2. Build a repertoire of strategies for sharing learning goals with students.

Preparation

1. The facilitator should be familiar with and prepared to lead the session.
2. The facilitator should make copies of the following article: Sato, M., & Atkin, J.M. (2006-2007, December-January). Supporting change in classroom assessment. *Educational Leadership, 64*(4), 76-79.
3. One or more volunteers should be ready to present their Classroom Connections activities, reflections, and evidence (including student work) to the group for discussion. All participants should be ready to contribute insights from their own Classroom Connections work.

Handout 2.1
Session 2 Agenda

Introduction (The facilitator leads this section.)

- The facilitator reviews the roles and expectations for the meeting.
- The facilitator reviews the agenda for the day.

Review Homework from Previous Topic (What is Formative Assessment?)

- The discussion leader shares and reflects on the group's experiences with Classroom Connections for Formative Assessment, reviews student work, and leads the group discussion (see pp. 21 and 22–23).

Introduce New Topic (Sharing Goals for Students' Learning)

- The facilitator introduces the new topic and distributes the Sharing Goals for Students' Learning handout on p. 27 and the Shared Language worksheet on p. 28.
- The facilitator distributes copies of the article "Supporting change in classroom assessment." All group members will read the article and write down their thoughts using the Reflections on Reading worksheet on p. 29 before the next meeting.
- All group members will make a commitment to try a few of the classroom activities (see pp. 30 or 31). The group will also decide who will present their findings at the next meeting.
- If pairs are not permanent features of your PLC, the group will identify who will work with whom for classroom trials.

Wrap-up (The facilitator leads this section.)

- Each member of the group will discuss what he or she learned.

Next Meeting Information

Handout 2.2
Sharing Goals for Students' Learning

Always share your goals for students' learning and check for students' understanding. Don't ask students, "Do you understand?" (They'll say yes, of course!) Instead, use strategies that help you assess students' comprehension of the meaning of learning goals and their comprehension of what good work looks like.

Help students give you information on what they understand about the assignment and the learning target. Use this information to affirm students' understanding and clarify misconceptions. Develop written strategies that can be used for review and reference in the future. You can also do the following:

- Ask students what questions they have about the assignment.
- For younger students, use pictures that show what they will do or what they will need for the assignment (e.g., a crystal ball for thoughts about an assignment or a pair of scissors for required tools for the assignment). Student-written words can be used with the pictures as appropriate. Colored pictures can be used as cover sheets for student folders.
- Use the K and W columns of a K-W-L Chart.
- Develop planning charts for individual or group work. Students must identify what needs to be done before they can plan how to do it.
- Describe the assignment or learning target. Ask students to describe what prior school experiences, outside school experiences, attitudes, and knowledge they already have. Check for relevance and use the information to adjust instruction.

Help students give you information on what they understand about the criteria for good work. Use this information to affirm students' understanding and clarify their misconceptions. Some examples you can use include the following:

- **Examples of student work.** Ask students to sort the work into good, medium, and not good piles and allow them to describe the characteristics of each. Use anonymous pieces from previous or fictional students.
- **Student-generated rubrics.** Research suggests young children's first attempts at rubrics might overweight neatness and appearance and underweight substance, but this can make a teachable moment. Students as young as 1st grade can help to create rubrics.
- **Student translations of teacher rubrics.** Ask students to rewrite teacher-made rubrics in their own words. This process supports students' comprehension of the rubrics and helps students create a kid-friendly guide for performance.

Worksheet 2.1
Shared Language: What is the Relationship Between Rubrics and Formative Assessment?

Definition

What does the term *rubrics* mean to you? How are *rubrics* related to formative assessment?

What do you wonder about *rubrics*?

Example and counterexample

Give an example of something you would consider a formative use of *rubrics*. Explain why.

Give an example of something you would not consider a formative use of *rubrics*. Explain why.

Sharing and focusing

With a partner, share your definitions, examples, and counterexamples. How did you fine-tune your ideas about *rubrics* based on your discussion?

In the whole group, share the results of your partner discussions. As a group, discuss and decide on the role of *rubrics* in formative assessment and write it below.

Worksheet 2.2
Reflections on Reading: Sharing Goals for Students' Learning

Read the article "Supporting change in classroom assessment." Answer the reflection questions individually and take your answers to your next PLC session to share your thoughts.

The authors write about a professional development and research project in formative assessment in science. The teachers in this article, Joni, Vicki, Tracey, and Elaine, show examples of strategies for sharing goals for students' learning.

1. What did you learn about sharing goals for students' learning from Joni Gilbertson's story? What did you learn about other aspects of formative assessment from Joni's example?

2. What did you learn about sharing goals for students' learning from Vicki Baker's story? What did you learn about other aspects of formative assessment from Vicki's example?

3. What did you learn about sharing goals for students' learning from Tracey Liebig's story? What did you learn about other aspects of formative assessment from Tracey's example?

4. What did you learn about sharing goals for students' learning from Elaine Fong's story? What did you learn about other aspects of formative assessment from Elaine's example?

5. What interested you the most about this article?

Reference

Sato, M., & Atkin, J.M. (2006-2007, December-January). Supporting change in classroom assessment. *Educational Leadership*, 64(4), 76-79.

Worksheet 2.3
Classroom Connections: Sharing Goals
Introductory Level

1. Select a learning goal that you are going to teach and write it in whatever format you use for your regular lesson plans. Then, write it in language that students would understand. Share this version with students.

2. Do a think-pair-share activity with your students. Divide your students into pairs and ask them to do the following (a) explain what they think they are going to learn in their own words, (b) explain why they think it is important, and (c) figure out at least one previous lesson topic that is related to this goal. In a whole-class discussion, have the student pairs share and discuss their answers and come to a class consensus for the three questions.

3. Teach your lesson. Collect evidence on what happens and appropriately document (a) what the students learned, (b) why they thought it was important, and (c) how students related this lesson with their previous learning. Evidence from your lesson can be student work samples, observations of student learning behavior (e.g., Are students focused? Are they staying on task?), student reflections or comments, or peer observation. What evidence did you collect, and what did it show?

4. What did you learn about your teaching? What do you still want to know?

Worksheet 2.4
Classroom Connections: Sharing Goals
Experienced Level

1. Select a learning goal for a performance (e.g., essays, book reports, lab reports, written answers to study questions). Share four to six examples of work from all levels of achievement, from good to poor. If you don't have real examples from previous students, construct teacher-made examples to illustrate the range of possible performance. If you are using a rubric, use at least one example per level. Present examples that represent levels of quality rather than quantity.

2. Divide your students into pairs and ask them to sort the work samples in order from good through poor. Ask them to explain why they put the examples in a specific order. Also, encourage your students to describe what is good about the good examples and what is weak or incomplete in the poor ones. Then, allow the pairs to share their thoughts in a whole-class discussion, and lead your class toward creating whole-group consensus on the work samples.

3. Teach your lesson and give the assignment to students. Collect evidence on what happens and appropriately document (a) what the students learned and (b) how they used information from the examples in their own performance. Evidence from your lesson can be student work samples, observations of student learning behavior (e.g., Are students focused? Are they staying on task?), student reflections or comments, or peer observation. What evidence did you collect, and what did it show?

4. What did you learn about your teaching? What do you still want to know?

Introduction

Students need opportunities to express their understanding (i.e., where they are) as they work in the classroom. They also need opportunities to learn how to express their understanding. If you just ask, "Do you understand?" many students will either say, "Yes" or "I have no clue." This topic area is about soliciting specific information from students so they are able to articulate their understanding. The teacher's role, in addition to soliciting the information, is helping students interpret what they understand. As the teacher, you know how students will work with a learning goal, how students' understanding develops, and how to chunk the task into smaller, meaningful bites as needed.

Goals for Session 3

1. Recognize the role of student understanding in the formative assessment process.
2. Build a repertoire of strategies for soliciting information from students about their understanding.

Preparation

1. The facilitator should be familiar with and prepared to lead the session.
2. The facilitator should make copies of the following article: Chappuis, J. (2005, November). Helping students understand assessment. *Educational Leadership*, 63(3),39-43.
3. All participants should be ready to discuss the reading from the previous session.
4. One or more volunteers should be ready to present their Classroom Connections activities, reflections, and evidence (including student work) to the group for discussion. All participants should be ready to contribute insights from their own Classroom Connections work.

Handout 3.1
Session 3 Agenda

Introduction (The facilitator leads this section.)

- The facilitator reviews the roles and expectations for the meeting.
- The facilitator reviews the agenda for the day.

Review Homework from Previous Topic (Sharing Goals for Student Learning)

- All participants will discuss the reading and share their responses from the Reflections on Reading worksheet on p. 29.
- The discussion leader shares and reflects on the group's experiences with Classroom Connections for Sharing Goals, reviews student work, and leads the group discussion (see pp. 30 and 31).

Introduce New Topic (Listening to Students)

- The facilitator introduces the new topic and distributes the Listening to Students handout on pp. 35–36 and the Shared Language worksheet on p. 37.
- The facilitator distributes copies of the article "Helping students understand assessment." All group members will read the article and write down their thoughts using the Reflections on Reading worksheet on p. 38 before the next meeting.
- All group members will make a commitment to try a few of the classroom activities (see pp. 39 or 40). The group will also decide who will present their findings at the next meeting.
- If pairs are not permanent features of your group, identify who will work with whom for classroom trials.

Wrap-up (The facilitator leads this section.)

- Each member of the group will discuss what he or she learned.

Next Meeting Information

Handout 3.2
Listening to Students

Ask students to give you information about what they understand and where they get stuck during an assignment. Use this information to affirm students' understanding and clarify misconceptions in a just-in-time fashion (i.e., the student gets the information just when he or she is thinking about it and needs it). Teachers can help students identify their understanding by using the following tools:

- **Happy/sad face or red/green light cards**. Students can have a set of these cards at their desks and use them to indicate their understanding.
- **Multiple-choice questions**. Students can have a set of cards at their desk with the letters A, B, C, and D. The students can hold up cards to allow teachers to check their understanding on multiple-choice items. Follow-up activities can include calling on students to explain the reason for their choice or grouping students to try to "convince" others of their answer. For younger children, a variation of this strategy is to use true/false or yes/no questions and hand-raising or standing by the desk (e.g., "Stand up if you think the cork will float.")
- **Whiteboards**. Students can use whiteboards to write down their answers.
- **Recipe boxes**. For memory facts like alphabet, color, and math facts, students can keep 3x5 index cards in a recipe box. The recipe box can help students organize their facts into different sections (e.g., fast, slow; easy, medium, hard) and track their understanding (e.g., students can have separate sections for known and unknown facts, and students can see how their knowledge progresses over time as they move the cards). Students own and use the box for their own enrichment. The box should not be used for grading.
- **Most and least clear cards**. Students can use these cards to identify their most and least clear points after a lesson. Collect the cards and use the information to adjust your instruction. You can also call the cards "The sticking point" or "One thing I'm sure I know" or "One thing I'd like to know more about."
- **Notes organizers or concept maps**. Students can use visual organizers to identify main and subordinate points in a chapter.

Help students give you information about their progress and understanding during a project. Use this information to affirm students' understanding, clarify misconceptions, and keep student work on track. Teachers can track students' understanding by using the following tools:

- **Work planners or logs**. Use work planners or logs with your students and help them track their progress by using a timeframe or counting the number of steps required for a particular report or project.

- **Mini-assessments.** Build in mini-assessments along the way for a large project. For example, for a big report, students can turn in a plan, an outline, or a brief essay based on their thesis. Provide an ungraded review and feedback to help students make the final product better.

Worksheet 3.1
Shared Language: What is a Misconception?

Definition

What does the term *misconception* mean to you? How is it related to formative assessment?

What do you wonder about *misconceptions?* How could formative assessment help you and your students gain more knowledge about *misconceptions?*

Example and counterexample

Give an example of something you would consider a *misconception.* Explain why.

Give an example of something you would not consider a *misconception.* Explain why.

Sharing and focusing

With a partner, share your definitions, examples, and counterexamples. How did you fine-tune your concept of *misconception* based on your discussion? What is the role of formative assessment in helping you and your students understand *misconceptions?*

In the whole group, share the results of your partner discussions. As a group, discuss and decide on a current working definition of *misconception* and write it below.

Worksheet 3.2
Reflections on Reading: Listening to Students

Read the article "Helping students understand assessment." Answer the reflection questions individually and take your answers to your next PLC session to share your thoughts.

1. The first part of the article describes the tension between teachers' responsibility for creating opportunities for learning and students' needs to feel capable of taking advantage of those opportunities. Reflect on your own experiences around this tension.

2. The authors present seven strategies for improving the formative assessment process. Select one of the strategies that you feel is particularly useful for helping students (a) understand a learning goal in an area you teach, (b) recognize their own skill level in relation to the goal, and (c) take responsibility for improvement.

3. Describe how you would customize this one strategy for use with a learning goal in your classroom. Explain how this strategy would allow you to get information from students about their understandings, misunderstandings, and their next-step learning needs.

4. What interested you the most about this article?

Reference

Chappuis, J. (2005, November). Helping students understand assessment. *Educational Leadership, 63*(3),39-43.

Worksheet 3.3
Classroom Connections: Listening to Students
Introductory Level

1. Select the student indicator system most appropriate for your content area and grade level (e.g., happy/sad face, traffic lights). Use the indicator system for your next direct instruction or seat work activity. Have students use happy or green when they understand and sad or red when they are confused or stuck in their work. Depending on the context, either stop and help the student or get a fellow student using a happy or green indicator to help the student who needs help. The goal is to use a mechanism for students to indicate confusion so they can get help in a just-in-time fashion. You may have to do this several times so students learn the system and get comfortable with it.

2. Collect evidence on what happens and appropriately document (a) what the students learned and (b) how they used information from the formative activity in their own performance. Evidence from your lesson can be student work samples, observations of student learning behavior (e.g., Are students focused? Are they staying on task?), student reflections or comments, or peer observation. What evidence did you collect, and what did it show?

3. What did you learn about your teaching? What do you still want to know?

Worksheet 3.4
Classroom Connections: Listening to Students
Experienced Level

1. Prepare sets of multiple-choice indicator cards for each student. Each card should read A, B, C, D, and so on. Prepare formative assessment questions with multiple-choice answers. Create the questions ahead of time and make sure they require reasoning as well as knowledge of facts and concepts. Use the questions at appropriate points in your lesson to survey the room about the level of understanding. Call on students to defend their answer choices and explain their reasoning. Alternatively, pair up students with different answer choices and allow the pairs to present agreed-on answers and reasoning to the class.

2. Explain to the students that wrong answers at this point are good because they give students opportunities to clarify understanding. Do not count these answers as a grade and be careful to treat all answers as information not evaluation. If it isn't safe to answer these questions in front of classmates, the activity will not work. You may need to use this strategy several times before the students get used to it.

3. Collect evidence on what happens and appropriately document (a) what the students learned and (b) how they used information from the formative activity in their own performance. Evidence from your lesson can be student work samples, observations of student learning behavior (e.g., Are students focused? Are they staying on task?), student reflections or comments, or peer observation. What evidence did you collect, and what did it show?

4. What did you learn about your teaching? What do you still want to know?

Session 4
Providing Effective Feedback

Introduction

Feedback is one of the most important components of formative assessment. It is the lynchpin in the three formative questions (i.e., "Where am I going?" "Where am I now?" and "What do I do next?"). Effective feedback helps students understand where they are now and what to do next. Not all feedback is effective. General praise doesn't help students understand these questions. Student feedback is best when it is descriptive, timely, and expressed in terms of criteria for good work. Feedback should also be given in a tone that suggests that the student is an active learner and not a passive follower of directions.

Goals for Session 4

1. Understand recommended choices about providing effective feedback on student work.
2. Develop skills for giving effective feedback.

Preparation

1. The facilitator should be familiar with and prepared to lead the session.
2. The facilitator should make copies of the following article: Brookhart, S. M. (2007-2008, December-January). Feedback that fits. *Educational Leadership*, 65(4),54-59.
3. All participants should be ready to discuss the reading from the previous session.
4. One or more volunteers should be ready to present their Classroom Connections activities, reflections, and evidence (including student work) to the group for discussion. All participants should be ready to contribute insights from their own Classroom Connections work.

Handout 4.1
Session 4 Agenda

Introduction (The facilitator leads this section.)

- The facilitator reviews the roles and expectations for the meeting.
- The facilitator reviews the agenda for the day.

Review Homework from Previous Topic (Listening to Students)

- All participants will discuss the reading and share their responses from the Reflections on Reading worksheet on p. 38.
- The discussion leader shares and reflects on the group's experiences with Classroom Connections for Listening to Students, reviews student work, and leads the group discussion (see pp. 39 and 40).

Introduce New Topic (Providing Effective Feedback)

- The facilitator introduces the new topic and distributes the Providing Effective Feedback handout on p. 43 and the Shared Language worksheet on p. 44.
- The facilitator distributes copies of the article "Feedback that fits." All group members will read the article and write down their thoughts using the Reflections on Reading worksheet on p. 45 before the next meeting.
- All group members will make a commitment to try a few of the classroom activities (see pp. 46 or 47). The group will also decide who will present their findings at the next meeting.
- If pairs are not permanent features of your group, identify who will work with whom for classroom trials.

Wrap-up (The facilitator leads this section.)

- Each member of the group will discuss what he or she learned.

Next Meeting Information

Handout 4.2
Providing Effective Feedback

As you think about providing feedback to your students, consider the following list to help you make good choices. Take into account both the students and the content. No one recommendation is right for every occasion. A few aspects to keep in mind as you provide feedback to your students include the following:

Timing of Feedback

- Give feedback as immediately as possible, especially for facts (e.g., right or wrong)

Amount of Feedback

- Prioritize and pick the most important points for each assignment
- Choose points that relate to major learning goals
- Consider each student's developmental level

Focus

- Describe the work and the process that students use for an assignment
- Do not evaluate students personally (e.g., as smart or dumb)

Criteria

- Compare student performance with the criteria for good work as set forth in the learning goals

Valence

- Use positive comments to describe work that is done well
- Accompany negative descriptions of the work with positive suggestions for improvement

Clarity

- Use words that the student will understand
- Be explicit

Specificity

- Use feedback that is specific enough that students will know what to do next but not so specific that it's done for them
- Identify errors or types of errors but avoid correcting every one

Tone

- Choose words that communicate respect for students and their work
- Choose words that position the student as the agent
- Choose words that cause students to think or wonder

Worksheet 4.1
Shared Language: What is Feedback?

Definition

What does the term *feedback* mean to you?

What do you wonder about *feedback?*

Example and counterexample

Give an example of something you would consider *feedback*. Explain why.

Give an example of something you would not consider *feedback*. Explain why.

Sharing and focusing

With a partner, share your definitions, examples, and counterexamples. How did you fine-tune your concept of *feedback* based on your discussion?

In the whole group, share the results of your partner discussions. As a group, discuss and decide on a current working definition of *feedback* and write it below.

Worksheet 4.2
Reflections on Reading: Providing Effective Feedback

Read the article "Feedback that fits." Answer the reflection questions individually and take your answers to your next PLC session to share your thoughts.

1. The author points out that the effectiveness of feedback depends on how students hear it. Have you ever checked to see what your students understand about your feedback? Does your feedback empower your students? If so, describe this event. If not, plan a way to try this in your classroom.

2. Reflect on the feedback you usually give to students in your classroom. On the basis of the suggestions in this article, select one aspect of your own feedback you want to work on. Explain your choice and describe what you want to try. Most important, describe how you will know what effect your feedback has on your students.

3. Think about feedback you have given to reluctant or struggling learners in your class. How do you remain positive for these students, and how do you decide what small, next steps to suggest for them?

4. Think about feedback you have given to successful learners in your class. Do you suggest next steps for expanding learning for students who have achieved the learning goals on the assignment? If not, what sort of feedback do you give them and what do they do with it?

5. What interested you the most about this article?

Reference

Brookhart, S. M. (2007-2008, December-January). Feedback that fits. *Educational Leadership*, 65(4), 54-59.

Worksheet 4.3
Classroom Connections: Feedback
Introductory Level

1. Select an assignment in which you provided written feedback to students. If all your feedback is oral (e.g., if you teach very young children), write down what you said or use peer observer notes. Using the recommendations on p. 43, comment on the nature of your feedback. Describe the timing, amount, focus, criteria, valence, clarity, specificity, and tone of your feedback. In your examples, include feedback that you have given to successful and struggling students.

2. After analyzing your feedback, select an aspect of feedback you want to focus on and improve for your next assignment. After the next assignment, describe the timing, amount, focus, criteria, valence, clarity, specificity, and tone in this round of feedback. Include feedback that you have given to successful and struggling students.

3. Collect evidence on what happens and appropriately document (a) what the students learned and (b) how they used feedback to improve their performance. Evidence can be student work samples, observations of student learning behavior (e.g., focus, being on task), student reflections or comments, and/or peer observation. What evidence did you collect, and what did it show?

4. What did you learn about your teaching? What do you still want to know?

Worksheet 4.4
Classroom Connections: Feedback
Experienced Level

1. Prepare a case study about how you used feedback for one of your assignments. Describe what you wanted the students to learn and how the assignment shows their learning. Select one or two successful students and one or two struggling students for your analysis. Analyze their work, the feedback you gave them, and why you gave specific feedback for each student. Use the categories on p. 43 for your analysis.

2. Next, follow the same students in their next assignment on a similar learning target. What opportunities did they have to use the information in your feedback? Was the feedback useful? If so, how? Evidence from your lesson can be student work samples from the next assignment (e.g.., using the previous feedback), observations of student learning behavior (e.g., Are students focused? Are they staying on task?), student reflections or comments, or peer observation. What evidence did you collect, and what did it show? Repeat this step if there are additional related assignments.

3. What did you learn about your teaching? What do you still want to know?

Session 5
Asking Questions that Encourage Students to Think

Introduction

You are probably familiar with questioning techniques such as using wait time or open-ended questions as instructional strategies. In this section, we are interested in using the information from these questions to learn more about what students understand. This knowledge will help you and your students discover what they understand, improve their learning skills, and identify next steps for achieving their learning goals.

Goals for Session 5

1. Understand the role of student discourse and use effective questions to stimulate students' thinking during the formative assessment process.
2. Develop skills for using questioning strategies that encourage students to think.

Preparation

1. The facilitator should be familiar with and prepared to lead the session.
2. The facilitator should make copies of the following article: Leahy, S., Lyon, C., Thompson, M., & Wiliam, D. (2005, November). Classroom assessment: Minute by minute, day by day. *Educational Leadership*, 63(3),18-24.
3. All participants should be ready to discuss the reading from the previous session.
4. One or more volunteers should be ready to present their Classroom Connections activities, reflections, and evidence (including student work) to the group for discussion. All participants should be ready to contribute insights from their own Classroom Connections work.

Handout 5.1
Session 5 Agenda

Introduction (The facilitator leads this section.)

- The facilitator reviews the roles and expectations for the meeting.
- The facilitator reviews the agenda for the day.

Review Homework from Previous Topic (Providing Effective Feedback)

- All participants will discuss the reading and share their responses from the Reflections on Reading worksheet on p. 45.
- The discussion leader shares and reflects on the group's experiences with Classroom Connections for Providing Effective Feedback, reviews student work, and leads the group discussion (see pp. 46 and 47).

Introduce New Topic (Asking Questions that Encourage Students to Think)

- The facilitator introduces the new topic and distributes the Asking Questions that Encourage Students to Think handout on p. 51 and the Shared Language worksheet on p. 52.
- The facilitator distributes copies of the article "Classroom assessment: Minute by minute, day by day." All group members will read the article and write down their thoughts using the Reflections on Reading worksheet on p. 53 before the next meeting.
- All group members will make a commitment to try a few of the classroom activities (see pp. 54 or 55). The group will also decide who will present their findings at the next meeting.

Wrap-up (The facilitator leads this section.)

- Each member of the group will discuss what he or she learned.

Next Meeting Information

Handout 5.2
Asking Questions that Encourage Students to Think

When you ask questions that encourage students to think, decide what knowledge and reasoning skills your students will need to achieve the learning target. These skills will be helpful as you create your questions. As you begin thinking about your questions, consider the following:

1. Ask open-ended questions rather than questions of fact.
   - Ask students to draw conclusions, formulate hypotheses, or make predictions.
   - Ask students to provide evidence for their claims and explain their reasoning.
   - Ask students to clarify, expand, or explain their own or others' points.

2. Do not respond to a student's answer by saying, "That's right" or "That's wrong." Instead, respond with another question or a comment of substance or ask other students to comment. Try to infer the student's understanding from his or her explanation.

3. Wait several seconds after asking a question before calling on a student. You might try one of the following strategies:
   - Enforce a no-hands-up rule after a question is asked, or ask students not to raise their hands until you ask them to do so. This process will give students time to think and will help them not to rush to get their "dibs in" for an answer.
   - Use a think-pair-share activity to ensure that students think about their responses and discuss them with a peer before speaking to the class.

4. Ask students to explain and respond to each other's points. Encourage students to actively listen to and ask questions from one another.

Worksheet 5.1
Shared Language: What Is an Open-ended Question?

Definition

What does the term *open-ended question* mean to you? How are *open-ended questions* related to formative assessment?

What do you wonder about *open-ended questions?*

Example and counterexample

Give an example of something you would consider an *open-ended question*. Explain why.

Give an example of something you would not consider an *open-ended question*. Explain why.

Sharing and focusing

With a partner, share your definitions, examples, and counterexamples. How did you fine-tune your concept of an *open-ended question* based on your discussion?

In the whole group, share the results of your partner discussions. As a group, discuss and decide on a current working definition of an *open-ended question* and write it below.

Worksheet 5.2
Reflections on Reading: Asking Questions that Encourage Students to Think

Read the article "Classroom assessment: Minute by minute, day by day." Answer the reflection questions individually and take your answers to your next PLC session to share your thoughts.

1. The authors present five strategies for formative assessment. The second strategy, engineering effective classroom discussions, questions, and learning tasks, is focused on asking questions that encourage students to think. Discuss how each of the five strategies helps teachers to encourage students to think.

2. How could you use "range-finding" questions in your classroom?

3. How could you use "hinge-point" questions in your classroom?

4. What other aspects of questioning do you use and find helpful (e.g., wait time, open-ended questions)? How do you use these questioning techniques in your teaching?

5. What interested you the most about this article?

Reference

Leahy, S., Lyon, C., Thompson, M., & Wiliam, D. (2005, November). Classroom assessment: Minute by minute, day by day. *Educational Leadership*, 63(3),18-24.

Worksheet 5.3
Classroom Connections: Questioning
Introductory Level

1. Select a learning target that lends itself to a classroom discussion. Prepare a set of relevant questions that require students to use their thinking and reasoning skills. Enforce a no-hands-up policy or use a think-pair-share activity to increase the wait time for responses and deepen student discussions. Tell the class how you will use this strategy and how it works. Explain to your students that the purpose of this assignment is to get them to think deeper and more completely.

2. Observe the amount and quality of class discussion around the questions. Note what you observe. How do these observations compare with your usual class discussion?

3. Collect evidence on what happens and appropriately document (a) what the students learned and (b) how they used information from the formative activity in their own performance. Evidence from your lesson can be student work samples, observations of student learning behavior (e.g., Are students focused? Are they staying on task?), student reflections or comments, or peer observation. What evidence did you collect, and what did it show?

4. What did you learn about your teaching? What do you still want to know?

Worksheet 5.4
Classroom Connections: Questioning
Experienced Level

1. Select a learning target that lends itself to a classroom discussion. Prepare a set of relevant questions that require students to use their thinking and reasoning skills. Explain to the class that they are to listen to each other's comments and ask further questions. Prepare a set of probing questions to keep the session going (e.g., "Who can explain in their own words the point George just made?" or "What would you like to ask Erica about her ideas?")

2. Sit back and serve as the facilitator for a student discussion. Observe the amount and quality of class discussion around the questions. Note what you observe. How do these observations compare with your usual class discussion?

3. Collect evidence on what happens and appropriately document (a) what the students learned and (b) how they used information from the formative activity in their own performance. Evidence from your lesson can be student work samples, observations of student learning behavior (e.g., Are students focused? Are they staying on task?), student reflections or comments, or peer observation. What evidence did you collect, and what did it show?

4. What did you learn about your teaching? What do you still want to know?

Session 6
Encouraging Student Self-Regulation

Introduction

Many teachers are familiar with the concept of self-efficacy — a student's perception that he or she can learn particular content or skills and will be successful in doing so. Self-regulation, however, is broader than that. Most self-regulated students have a degree of self-efficacy, but they also have a habit of making sure they attend to their learning progress. They check to make sure they understand what they are supposed to do, plan and monitor their own work as they do it, assess their own progress, know when they need to ask questions, and give themselves their own internal rewards for achievement. When teachers use formative assessment strategies well, they provide students with a model for using these strategies. Students gradually internalize the process. Self-regulation strategies can be taught, and they can be scaffolded for students who have difficulty learning them.

Goals for Session 6

1. Understand the concept of student self-regulation and its relationship to the formative assessment process.
2. Develop a repertoire of strategies that encourage student self-regulation.

Preparation

1. The facilitator should be familiar with and prepared to lead the session.
2. The facilitator should make copies of the following article: Saddler, B., & Andrade, H. (2004, October). The writing rubric. *Educational Leadership*, 62(2),48-52.
3. All participants should be ready to discuss the reading from the previous session.
4. One or more volunteers should be ready to present their Classroom Connections activities, reflections, and evidence (including student work) to the group for discussion. All participants should be ready to contribute insights from their own Classroom Connections work.

Handout 6.1
Session 6 Agenda

Introduction (The facilitator leads this section.)

- The facilitator reviews the roles and expectations for the meeting.
- The facilitator reviews the agenda for the day.

Review Homework from Previous Topic (Asking Questions that Encourage Students to Think)

- All participants will discuss the reading and share their responses from the Reflections on Reading worksheet on p. 53.
- The discussion leader shares and reflects on the group's experiences with Classroom Connections for Questioning, reviews student work, and leads the group discussion (see pp. 54 and 55).

Introduce New Topic (Encouraging Student Self-Regulation)

- The facilitator introduces the new topic and distributes the Encouraging Student Self-Regulation handout on pp. 59–60 and the Shared Language worksheet on p. 61.
- The facilitator distributes copies of the article "The writing rubric." All group members will read the article and write down their thoughts using the Reflections on Reading worksheet on p. 62 before the next meeting.
- All group members will make a commitment to try a few of the classroom activities (see pp. 63 or 64). The group will also decide who will present their findings at the next meeting.

Wrap-up (The facilitator leads this section.)

- Each member of the group will discuss what he or she learned.

Next Meeting Information

Handout 6.2
Encouraging Student Self-Regulation

Help students use information about their understanding and the quality of their work to set goals and organize their studying. Students can use the following strategies for self-regulation:

- **Charts and graphs.** Students can keep charts or graphs to keep track of their goals and reflect on their progress.
- **Self-evaluation.** Encourage students to evaluate their own work and set goals for what they want to do next to improve. Students can use rubrics to evaluate their work.
- **Practice test questions.** Allow your students to generate their own practice test questions. Give your students an outline that includes the content, number, and type of questions that will be the test. Ask them to write at least one fact question and one reasoning question for each area. Pool the questions together and allow your students to use them to study for a test.
- **Self-reflection sheets.** Students can use self-reflection sheets to help them study for a test. For example, students can create a self-reflection sheet that includes columns for what they understand ("I get it") or don't understand ("I don't get it") for an upcoming test. For the "I get it" column, students can plan to review those items before the test and for the "I don't get it" column, they can set aside time to learn the material.
- **Homework logs.** Students can use homework sheets or homework logs to help them keep track of the topic, time, place, and resources that they will need for an assignment.

For further learning, students can use the results from tests or projects and turn them into plans for self-regulation. Strategies that students can use include the following:

- **Create a list of missed questions.** Students make a list of test questions they got wrong on a test. The can categorize the questions by marking them as true mistakes (e.g., "I knew the answer, but I marked the wrong choice or made simple calculation error") or misconceptions (e.g., "I did not know the answer or I misunderstood the question"). When students follow-up on careless errors, they learn how to take their time, check their work, and be more careful; when they follow-up on misconceptions, they learn and clarify their misunderstandings.
- **Reflect on graded work and teacher feedback.** For projects or papers, students can reflect on their progress by reviewing their completed work, the rubrics or grading criteria for each assignment, and the teacher's feedback. Students can use these tools to help them identify gaps in their learning

and reflect on their next steps. They can also use this reflective work as an opportunity to ask teachers to redo an assignment.

- **Reflect on personal effort.** Ask students to assess different aspects of their effort. If you just ask students, "How much effort did you put into this assignment?," most students will simply tell you how much time they spent on their work. Instead, ask questions such as, "How hard did you concentrate?" "How carefully did you work?" "How did you handle new ideas or aspects of the assignment?" and "How much help did you need, and did you ask for it?" Then, students can reflect on these questions individually, with the teacher, or in small groups. Students can use this information for the next project or assignment.

Worksheet 6.1
Shared Language: What is Self-Regulation?

Definition

What does the term *student self-regulation* mean to you?

What do you wonder about *student self-regulation?*

Example and counterexample

Give an example of something you would consider *student self-regulation*. Explain why.

Give an example of something you would not consider *student self-regulation*. Explain why.

Sharing and focusing

With a partner, share your definitions, examples, and counterexamples. How did you fine-tune your concept of *student self-regulation* based on your discussion?

In the whole group, share the results of your partner discussions. As a group, discuss and decide on a current working definition of *student self-regulation* and write it below.

Worksheet 6.2
Reflections on Reading: Encouraging Student Self-Regulation

Read the article "The writing rubric." Answer the reflection questions individually and take your answers to your next PLC session to share your thoughts.

1. This article introduces us to two students, Maren and Katie. Maren has several self-regulation skills while Katie only has a few. Describe two students in your class who are similar to Maren and Katie.

2. This article also shows teachers how to use writing rubrics to foster good writing and self-regulation skills. How can you adapt these skills to other subject areas?

3. As illustrated by Mrs. Smith's work with Katie, self-regulation skills can be taught. Plan strategies you can use in your classroom to teach self-regulation skills to a whole class and an individual student.

4. What interested you the most about this article?

Reference

Saddler, B., & Andrade, H. (2004, October). The writing rubric. *Educational Leadership, 62*(2), 48-52.

Worksheet 6.3
Classroom Connections: Self-Regulation
Introductory Level

1. Select an assignment that requires students to perform. Distribute and use a rubric to score the assignment. When students have finished a draft of the assignment, ask them to assess their own work using the rubric. For each criterion on the rubric, ask students to select which level of quality they think describes their performance and explain why. If the assignment is a writing assignment, students can use highlighters to point out aspects of their text they think match the rubric descriptions. Then, ask students to revise their work based on their own evaluations. Explain what you will do here.

2. Collect evidence on what happens and appropriately document (a) what the students learned and (b) how they used information from their self-evaluation to improve their performance. Evidence from your lesson can be student work samples, observations of student learning behavior (e.g., Are students focused? Are they staying on task?), student reflections or comments, or peer observation. What evidence did you collect, and what did it show?

3. What did you learn about your teaching? What do you still want to know?

Worksheet 6.4
Classroom Connections: Self-Regulation
Experienced Level

1. Select a developmental learning target (e.g., writing or problem solving). Ask students to keep a journal and record their strengths and weaknesses regarding this target, set a goal for improvement, and plan a strategy or program to reach their goal. Students should write their plan and keep it with them. Give students time to work on their goals. Explain what you will do here.

2. Collect evidence on what happens and appropriately document (a) what the students learned and (b) how they used insights from their self-evaluation, goal-setting, and planning. Evidence from your lesson can be student work samples, observations of student learning behavior (e.g., Are students focused? Are they staying on task?), student reflections or comments, or peer observation. What evidence did you collect, and what did it show?

3. What did you learn about your teaching? What do you still want to know?

Using Formative Assessment Information in Instructional Planning

Introduction

Using formative assessment information in instructional planning is the last topic area in this PLC study guide. Thus far, we have focused on student involvement in formative assessment. We hope this will counter the common misconception that formative assessment is *only* about teacher instructional planning. However, information from formative assessment can and should help teachers decide how much time to devote in each area and what concepts and skills to review, reteach, or expand in their lessons.

Goals for Session 7

1. Understand the role of formative assessment information in instructional planning.
2. Develop a repertoire of strategies for using formative assessment information in instructional planning.

Preparation

1. The facilitator should be familiar with and prepared to lead the session.
2. The facilitator should make copies of the following article: Shephard, L.A. (2005, November). Linking formative assessment to scaffolding. *Educational Leadership*, 63(3),66-70.
3. All participants should be ready to discuss the reading from the previous session.
4. One or more volunteers should be ready to present their Classroom Connections activities, reflections, and evidence (including student work) to the group for discussion. All participants should be ready to contribute insights from their own Classroom Connections work.

*Note: If this is the last session before the evaluation session, a complete discussion of the new reading and new Classroom Connections work may not be possible. The group may wish to arrange a separate meeting before the final evaluation session.

Handout 7.1
Session 7 Agenda

Introduction (The facilitator leads this section.)

- The facilitator reviews the roles and expectations for the meeting.
- The facilitator reviews the agenda for the day.

Review Homework from Previous Topic (Encouraging Student Self-Regulation)

- All participants will discuss the reading and share their responses from the Reflections on Reading worksheet on p. 62.
- The discussion leader shares and reflects on the group's experiences with Classroom Connections for Self-Regulation, reviews student work, and leads the group discussion (see pp. 63 and 64).

Introduce New Topic (Using Formative Assessment Information in Instructional Planning)

- The facilitator introduces the new topic and distributes the Using Formative Assessment Information in Instructional Planning handout on pp. 67–68 and the Shared Language worksheet on p. 69.
- The facilitator distributes copies of the article "Linking formative assessment to scaffolding." All group members will read the article and write down their thoughts using the Reflections on Reading worksheet on p. 70 before the next meeting.
- All group members will make a commitment to try a few of the classroom activities (see pp. 71 or 72). The group will also decide who will present their findings at the next meeting.

Wrap-up (The facilitator leads this section.)

- Each member of the group will discuss what he or she learned.

Next Meeting Information

Handout 7.2
Using Formative Assessment Information in Instructional Planning

Most of this book is focused on developing formative assessment practices that help students articulate their progress against clear goals, develop self-regulation skills, and improve their studying and learning strategies. These aspects of formative assessment are typically more difficult to understand than formative assessment practices that help teachers adjust instruction. Using formative assessment information to improve your instructional strategies is also important, and we conclude with a session to help you develop these skills. Many districts ask teachers to use the results of state or benchmark tests formatively in planning instruction. Information from classroom formative assessments is useful both for fine-tuning day-to-day instruction and for supplementing state or benchmark test information for instructional planning. Teachers can use state or benchmark test results formatively in instructional planning as follows:

- Identify the standards that are areas of strength and weakness for students
- Use classroom formative assessment methods to analyze specific weaknesses and student misunderstandings. Give students assignments that focus on an area of weakness and observe their work and their process. Use the diagnostic information from state tests and classroom formative assessments to plan for next steps in instruction. Teachers should use the next steps to give students effective feedback and remediate areas of misconception.
- Use classroom formative assessment methods to discover students' special interests or areas of strength. Teachers can help students enrich and expand these skills during the next steps in instruction.

* Note: Most state or large-scale test results will not provide fine-grained information that teachers can use for targeted lesson plans. However, they can use the test results with classroom formative assessment to identify and plan for students' learning needs.

Teachers can use results from classroom formative assessment in instructional planning as follows:

- Observe students' work and the processes they use.
- Compare the quality of student work and how students work toward a specific learning goal. Are students stuck on a misconception? Are they missing a step in the process? Do they understand how a specific skill fits with other things they have learned?) Conversely, do students have special interests or skills that go above and beyond a specific learning goal?

- For areas of weakness, plan next steps in instruction that provide effective feedback, remediate areas of misconception, and give students tools for additional practice and self-assessment.
- For areas of special interest or strength, plan next steps in instruction that enrich and expand students' interests and skills.

Teachers can use formative assessment information to group students for instruction as follows:

- Create remediation groups that are flexible and temporary. Students should not get stuck in or become stigmatized by a group.
- Use formative assessment information to form flexible, heterogeneous groups. Teachers can use the power of cooperative learning to help advance students' learning.

Worksheet 7.1
Shared Language: What is Diagnosis?

Definition

What does the term *diagnosis* mean to you?

What do you wonder about *diagnosis?*

Example and counterexample

Give an example of something you would consider a *diagnosis*. Explain why.

Give an example of something you would not consider a *diagnosis*. Explain why.

Sharing and focusing

With a partner, share your definitions, examples, and counterexamples. How did you fine-tune your concept of *diagnosis* based on your discussion?

In the whole group, share the results of your partner discussions. As a group, discuss and decide on a current working definition of *diagnosis* and write it below.

Worksheet 7.2
Reflections on Reading: Using Formative Assessment Information in Instructional Planning

Read the article "Linking formative assessment to scaffolding." Answer the reflection questions individually and take your answers to your next PLC session to share your thoughts.

1. What is the relationship between instructional planning and scaffolding?

2. How does formative assessment information from students affect how teachers use scaffolding?

3. The author discusses four strategies—eliciting prior knowledge, providing effective feedback, teaching for transfer of knowledge, and teaching students how to self-assess—that are common to both formative assessment and scaffolding. Select one of these strategies and discuss how you could use it in a specific lesson in your classroom.

4. What interested you the most about this article?

Reference

Shephard, L.A. (2005, November). Linking formative assessment to scaffolding. *Educational Leadership, 63*(3),66-70.

Worksheet 7.3
Classroom Connections: Instructional Planning
Introductory Level

1. Obtain and review whole-class and student-level results for your state or benchmark test. If possible, find out how many test items per standard objective. What information do you find that could be useful for your instructional planning?

2. What additional information will you need about student knowledge, misconceptions, and specific skills in order to make lesson plans for remediation? Decide how you will obtain this information. (If you teach a subject for which there is no standardized test information, such as music or visual arts, start here.)

3. Using the information from both large-scale and classroom level assessment, create specific lessons plans that address areas of weaknesses or remediation. Describe what you will do.

4. After instruction, collect evidence on student achievement based on the standards and specific learning targets of interest. Evidence from your lesson can be student work samples, observations of student learning behavior (e.g., Are students focused? Are they staying on task?), student reflections or comments, or peer observation. What evidence did you collect, and what did it show?

5. What did you learn about your teaching? What do you still want to know?

Worksheet 7.4
Classroom Connections: Instructional Planning
Experienced Level

1. Do a case study on an instructional intervention you did based on state or large-scale test data and classroom formative assessment information. What information did you focus on from the state test? What additional information did you collect from classroom formative assessment? What did you conclude about student learning needs?

2. Describe the instructional intervention. What did you enhance, repeat, or change? Were students involved in your instructional intervention? If so, how?

3. What were students' responses to this instructional intervention?

4. After instruction, collect evidence on student achievement based on the standards and specific learning targets of interest. Evidence from your lesson can be student work samples, observations of student learning behavior (e.g., Are students focused? Are they staying on task?), student reflections or comments, or peer observation. What evidence did you collect, and what did it show?

5. What did you learn about teaching from this assessment information? How can you use this information for planning instructional intervention? What would you do differently next time? What aspects of this process would you repeat?

Section III

What Did We Learn?

Set aside at least one session to reflect on what you and your professional learning community learned.

Preparation

In preparation for this session, complete the Post-Assessment Questionnaire on pp. 75–76. Locate the Pre-Assessment Questionnaire you completed for Session 1. Complete the Pre- and Post-Assessment Comparison on pp. 77–78.

Materials

Bring your journal and any other artifacts from your work that you wish to discuss.

Agenda

At this session, you and your group can complete one or all of the following activities:

1. Share journal entries or any insights from the school year in an open discussion. Choose a recorder to take notes from the meeting on newsprint, a blackboard, or a laptop.
2. Share insights from your responses to the Key Questions about Professional Learning in Formative Assessment worksheet on p. 79.
   a. Group members will complete the worksheet on p. 79 and begin thinking about their responses.
   b. Each group member will choose a partner for think-pair-share discussion. Each pair will look for similarities and differences in their insights.
   c. Each pair will report out to the whole group. As a group, all members will review the responses and determine if there are any general conclusions that are common for the whole group. The group should also look for any interesting insights that are not shared by the whole group.

3. Plan for next steps.
   a. Does your group want to continue working in a PLC next year or next semester?
   b. Are there other teachers or administrators whom you might recruit for a similar professional learning group next year or next semester?
   c. Would any of the current members be interested in continuing as facilitators or more experienced peers?
   d. What logistical matters need to be planned in advance for the next learning group?

FIGURE 4

Post-Assessment Questionnaire

As you complete your professional learning community work in formative assessment, circle the choice that best represents how you feel about each topic. There are no right or wrong answers.

Using formative assessment in my regular classroom practice			
How much do I know about this?	a lot	a little	not much
How skilled am I at doing this?	very	somewhat	not very
How often do I do this?	routinely	sometimes	not often
How important is this to me?	very	somewhat	not very
How interested am I in learning more about this?	very	somewhat	not very
Setting and sharing goals for students' learning			
How much do I know about this?	a lot	a little	not much
How skilled am I at doing this?	very	somewhat	not very
How often do I do this?	routinely	sometimes	not often
How important is this to me?	very	somewhat	not very
How interested am I in learning more about this?	very	somewhat	not very
Soliciting and listening to students' comments, answers, questions, or problems related to learning goals			
How much do I know about this?	a lot	a little	not much
How skilled am I at doing this?	very	somewhat	not very
How often do I do this?	routinely	sometimes	not often
How important is this to me?	very	somewhat	not very
How interested am I in learning more about this?	very	somewhat	not very
Providing effective feedback on student work			
How much do I know about this?	a lot	a little	not much
How skilled am I at doing this?	very	somewhat	not very
How often do I do this?	routinely	sometimes	not often
How important is this to me?	very	somewhat	not very
How interested am I in learning more about this?	very	somewhat	not very
Asking questions that encourage students to think			
How much do I know about this?	a lot	a little	not much
How skilled am I at doing this?	very	somewhat	not very
How often do I do this?	routinely	sometimes	not often
How important is this to me?	very	somewhat	not very
How interested am I in learning more about this?	very	somewhat	not very

(con't)

Encouraging student self-regulation			
How much do I know about this?	a lot	a little	not much
How skilled am I at doing this?	very	somewhat	not very
How often do I do this?	routinely	sometimes	not often
How important is this to me?	very	somewhat	not very
How interested am I in learning more about this?	very	somewhat	not very
Using formative assessment information in instructional planning			
How much do I know about this?	a lot	a little	not much
How skilled am I at doing this?	very	somewhat	not very
How often do I do this?	routinely	sometimes	not often
How important is this to me?	very	somewhat	not very
How interested am I in learning more about this?	very	somewhat	not very

FIGURE 5

Pre- and Post-Assessment Comparison

Look at your pre- and post- assessment questionnaires. Use this worksheet to compare your assessments and to reflect on any changes you have made. Rate your responses on a scale of 1, 2, 3 (3 = a lot, 2 = a little, 1 = not much). List your pre- and post-assessment numbers and subtract to calculate the difference between the two numbers.

	POST-ASSESSMENT −	PRE-ASSESSMENT =	CHANGE

Using formative assessment in my regular classroom practice
Knowledge
Skill
Frequency
Importance
Interest

Setting and sharing goals for students' learning
Knowledge
Skill
Frequency
Importance
Interest

Soliciting and listening to students' comments, answers, questions, or problems related to learning goals
Knowledge
Skill
Frequency
Importance
Interest

Providing effective feedback on student work
Knowledge
Skill
Frequency
Importance
Interest

Asking questions that encourage students to think
Knowledge
Skill
Frequency
Importance
Interest

(con't)

Encouraging student self-regulation

Knowledge

Skill

Frequency

Importance

Interest

Using formative assessment information in instructional planning

Knowledge

Skill

Frequency

Importance

Interest

Finally, look for areas that changed in a positive direction and areas that changed in a negative direction. In the space below, interpret what these changes mean for you.

Worksheet 3.0
Key Questions about Professional Learning in Formative Assessment

Write your individual responses to these questions and include the reasons why you chose your answer. After you have reflected on your responses individually, share and discuss your thoughts with a partner. Finally, discuss these questions with the whole group. Where do you agree or disagree? What do the responses tell you about professional learning in formative assessment?

1. How well did our group function?
   a. How well did we work collaboratively?
   b. How deeply did we think, read, and discuss the session topics?
   c. How well did we present and examine evidence from the Classroom Connections?

2. To what degree did we achieve our shared goals?
   a. Did we help each teacher increase his or her knowledge and skill in formative assessment?
   b. Did we help each teacher increase student motivation and achievement in his or her classroom?

References and Web Links

References

Easton, L. B. (2008). From professional development to professional learning. *Phi Delta Kappan*, 89(10), 755-759, 761.

McLaughlin, M. W., & Talbert, J. E. (2006). *Building school-based teacher learning communities*. New York: Teachers College Press.

Web Links

Electronic versions of these articles
are available for download at **www.ascd.org/downloads.**

Enter this unique key to unlock the files:
109038

If you have difficulty accessing the files, e-mail webhelp@ascd.org or call
1-800-933-ASCD for assistance.

Brookhart, S. M. (2007-2008, December-January). Feedback that fits. *Educational Leadership*, 65, (4), 54-59. Available from http://www.ascd.org/publications/educational_leadership/dec07/vol65/num04/Feedback_That_Fits.aspx

Chappuis, J. (2005, November). Helping students understand assessment. *Educational Leadership*, 63 (3)39-43. Available from http://www.ascd.org/publications/educational_leadership/nov05/vol63/num03/Helping_Students_Understand_Assessment.aspx.

Chappuis, S., & Chappuis, J. (2007-2008, December-January). The best value in formative assessment. *Educational Leadership*, 65 (4), 14-18. Available from http://www.ascd.org/publications/educational_leadership/dec07/vol65/num04/The_Best_Value_in_Formative_Assessment.aspx

Leahy, S., Lyon, C., Thompson, M., & Wiliam, D. (2005, November). Classroom assessment: Minute by minute, day by day. *Educational Leadership*, 63(3), 18-24. Available from http://www.ascd.org/publications/educational_leadership/nov05/vol63/num03/Classroom_Assessment.aspx.

Saddler, B., & Andrade, H. (2004, October). The writing rubric. *Educational Leadership*, 62(2), 48-52. Available from http://www.ascd.org/publications/educational_leadership/oct04/vol62/num02/The_Writing_Rubric.aspx

Sato, M., & Atkin, J.M. (2006-2007, December-January). Supporting change in classroom assessment. *Educational Leadership*, 64 (4), 76-79. Available from http://www.ascd.org/publications/educational_leadership/dec06/vol64/num04/Supporting_Change_in_Classroom_Assessment.aspx

Shephard, L.A. (2005, November). Linking formative assessment to scaffolding. Educational Leadership, 63(3), 66-70. Available from http://www.ascd.org/publications/educational_leadership/nov05/vol63/num03/Linking_Formative_Assessment_to_Scaffolding.aspx.

About the Author

Susan M. Brookhart is an independent educational consultant based in Helena, Montana. She works with ASCD as an ASCD Faculty Member, providing onsite professional development in Formative Assessment. She has taught both elementary and middle school. She was Professor and Chair of the Department of Educational Foundations and Leadership at Duquesne University, where she currently serves as Senior Research Associate in the Center for Advancing the Study of Teaching and Learning. She serves on the state assessment advisory committees for Montana and Nebraska. She has been the Education columnist for *National Forum*, the journal of Phi Kappa Phi. She is the 2007–2009 editor of *Educational Measurement: Issues and Practice*, a journal of the National Council on Measurement in Education. She is author of *The Art and Science of Classroom Assessment and Grading* and *Formative Assessment Strategies for Every Classroom* (an ASCD Action Tool) and *How to Give Effective Feedback to Your Students*. She is coauthor of *Assessment and Grading in Classrooms* and *Educational Assessment of Students* (5th ed.). She has written or coauthored more than 40 articles on classroom assessment, teacher professional development, and evaluation and serves on the editorial boards of several journals. She received her Ph.D. in Educational Research and Evaluation from The Ohio State University.

Related ASCD Resources: Formative Assessment

At the time of publication, the following ASCD resources were available; for the most up to-date information about ASCD resources, go to www.ascd.org. ASCD stock numbers are noted in parentheses.

Mixed Media

Formative Assessment Strategies for Every Classroom: An ASCD Action Tool by Susan Brookhart (one three-ring binder) (#707010)

Print Products

Checking for Understanding: Formative Assessment Techniques for Your Classroom by Douglas Fisher and Nancy Frey (#107023)

How to Give Effective Feedback to Your Students by Susan Brookhart (#108019)

Transformative Assessment by W. James Popham (#108018)

Videos and DVDs

The power of formative assessment to advance learning. (three 30-minute DVDs with a comprehensive user guide) (#608067)

THE WHOLE CHILD The Whole Child Initiative helps schools and communities create learning environments that allow students to be healthy, safe, engaged, supported, and challenged. To learn more about other books and resources that relate to the whole child, visit www.wholechildeducation.org.

For additional resources, visit us on the World Wide Web (http://www.ascd.org), send an e-mail message to member@ascd.org, call the ASCD Service Center (1-800-933-ASCD or 703-578-9600, then press 2), send a fax to 703-575-5400, or write to Information Services, ASCD, 1703 N. Beauregard St., Alexandria, VA 22311-1714 USA.